ters,

Joy for the Heart

God knows no strangers, He loves us all,
The poor, the rich, the great, the small.
He is a Friend who is always there
To share our troubles and lessen our care.
No one is a stranger in God's sight,
For God is love and in His light
May we, too, try in our small way
To make new friends from day to day.

Whatever the celebration, whatever the day, whatever the event, whatever the occasion, Helen Steiner Rice possessed the ability to express the appropriate feeling for that particular moment in time.

A happening became happier, a sentiment more sentimental, a memory more memorable because of her deep sensitivity to put into understandable language the emotion being experienced. Her positive attitude, her concern for others, and her love of God are identifiable threads woven into her life, her work . . . and even her death.

Prior to her passing, she established the HELEN STEINER RICE FOUNDATION, a nonprofit corporation whose purpose is to award grants to worthy charitable programs that aid the elderly, the needy, and the poor. In her lifetime, these were the individuals about whom Mrs. Rice was greatly concerned.

Royalties from the sale of this book will add to the financial capabilities of the HELEN STEINER RICE FOUNDATION, thus making possible additional grants to various qualified, worthwhile, and charitable programs. Because of her foresight, her caring, and her deep convictions, Helen Steiner Rice continues to touch a countless number of lives. Thank you for your assistance in helping to keep Helen's dream alive.

Virginia J. Ruehlmann, Administrator
The Helen Steiner Rice Foundation
Suite 2100, Atrium Two
221 E. Fourth Street
Cincinnati, Ohio 45201

Joy for the Heart

Helen Steiner Rice

Compiled by Virginia J. Ruehlmann

HUTCHINSON

London

This edition first published in 1993 by
Hutchinson

Random House UK Ltd
20 Vauxhall Bridge Road, London SW1V 2SA

Random House Australia (Pty) Ltd
20 Alfred Street, Milsons Point, Sydney, NSW 2061, Australia

Random House New Zealand Ltd
18 Poland Road, Glenfield, Auckland 10, New Zealand

Random House South Africa (Pty) Ltd
PO Box 337, Bergvlei, South Africa

A CIP catalogue record is available from the British Library

Printed and bound by Tien Wah Press in Singapore

ISBN 0 09 178089 6

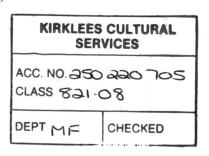

Dedicated to
All who have ever brought
or
will ever bring
joy to another's heart

Contents

But the fruit of the Spirit is love, joy, peace, patience, kindness, goodness, faithfulness, gentleness, self-control. . . .

Galatians 5:22, 23

Introduction

Joy for the heart springs from within. The very attributes that are enumerated as the fruit of the Spirit in Galatians 5:22, 23 are the inner qualities that will add joy to your soul.

We can find pleasure in God's creative handiwork, be it a multicolored sunrise or an iridescent crescent moon in the star-studded sky, a powerful, monochromatic waterfall or a clear, rippling brook. We can also derive enjoyment from a lilting strain of music, from kind words of encouragement, from heartfelt embraces, and from simple but sincere expressions of understanding.

Such acts serve as catalysts to cheerfulness, and each one becomes a joy for the heart. The pleasure originating from such experiences is transitory, but the memory of the reaction continues infinitely.

Adherence to a life-style that promotes a joyful atmosphere adds an inner degree of personal gladness and satisfaction.

The life and words of Helen Steiner Rice exemplify perseverance, provide inspiration, and offer encouragement on adding joy for the heart.

May this collection of poems and quotations serve to increase the joy-giving qualities in your life and, through your thoughts, words, and actions, spread into the lives of those around you.

Joyfully,

Virginia J. Ruehlmann

Joy for the Heart

God gives us a power we so seldom employ
For we're so unaware it is filled with such joy,
For the gift that God gives us is anticipation,
Which we can fulfill with sincere expectation.
For there's power in belief when we think we will find
Joy for the heart and sweet peace for the mind.
And believing the day will bring a surprise
Is not only pleasant but surprisingly wise,
For we open the door to let joy walk through
When we learn to expect the best and most, too,
And believing we'll find a happy surprise
Makes reality out of a fancied surmise!

Love

Love is patient and kind; love is not jealous or boastful; it is not arrogant or rude. Love does not insist on its own way; it is not irritable or resentful; it does not rejoice at wrong, but rejoices in the right. Love bears all things, believes all things, hopes all things, endures all things.

1 Corinthians 13:4–7

Let Daily Prayers Dissolve Your Cares

We all have cares and problems
   we cannot solve alone,
But if we go to God in prayer
   we are never on our own.
For there can be no failures
   or hopeless, unsaved sinners
If we enlist the help of God
   who makes all losers winners.
So meet Him in the morning
   and go with Him through the day
And thank Him for His guidance
   each evening when you pray,
And if you follow faithfully
   this daily way to pray
You will never in your lifetime
   face another hopeless day,
For like a soaring eagle
   you too can rise above
The storms of life around you
   on the wings of prayer and love.

But they who wait for the Lord shall renew their strength, they shall mount up with wings like eagles, they shall run and not be weary, they shall walk and not faint.

Isaiah 40:31

Everybody Everywhere Needs
Somebody Sometime

Everybody, everywhere,
    no matter what his station,
Has moments of deep loneliness
    and quiet desperation,
For this lost and lonely feeling
    is inherent in mankind—
It is just the spirit speaking
    as God tries again to find
An opening in the worldly wall
    man builds against God's touch,
For he feels so self-sufficient
    that he does not need God much,
So he vainly goes on struggling
    to find some explanation
For these disturbing, lonely moods
    of inner isolation.
But the answer keeps eluding him
    for in his selfish, finite mind
He does not even recognize
    that he cannot ever find

The reason for life's emptiness
　　unless he learns to share
The problems and the burdens
　　that surround him everywhere.
But when his eyes are opened
　　and he looks with love at others
He begins to see not strangers
　　but understanding brothers.
So open up your hardened hearts
　　and let God enter in—
He only wants to help you
　　a new life to begin.
And every day's a good day
　　to lose yourself in others
And anytime a good time
　　to see mankind as brothers,
And this can only happen
　　when you realize it's true
That everyone needs someone
　　and that someone is you!

What More Can You Ask?

God's love endureth forever—
What a wonderful thing to know
When the tides of life run against you
And your spirit is downcast and low.
God's kindness is ever around you,
Always ready to freely impart
Strength to your faltering spirit,
Cheer to your lonely heart.
God's presence is ever beside you,
As near as the reach of your hand,
You have but to tell Him your troubles,
There is nothing He won't understand.
And knowing God's love is unfailing,
And His mercy unending and great,
You have but to trust in His promise—
God comes not too soon or too late.
So wait with a heart that is patient
For the goodness of God to prevail,
For never do prayers go unanswered,
And His mercy and love never fail.

Blessed be the God and Father of our Lord Jesus Christ, the Father of mercies and God of all comfort, who comforts us in all our affliction, so that we may be able to comfort those who are in any affliction, with the comfort with which we ourselves are comforted by God.

2 Corinthians 1:3, 4

It Takes the Bitter and the Sweet

It takes the bitter and the sweet
  to make a life full and complete,
So when God sends
  some unwanted affliction,
Be assured that it comes
  with His kind benediction,
And if we accept it
  as a gift of His love,
We'll be showered with blessings
  from our Father above.
For His grace is sufficient,
  whatever betide us,
And it only takes faith
  to keep Him beside us.

Many are the afflictions of the righteous; but the Lord delivers him out of them all.

Psalm 34:19

Joy

If you keep my commandments, you will abide in my love, just as I have kept my Father's commandments and abide in his love. These things I have spoken to you, that my joy may be in you, and that your joy may be full.

John 15:10, 11

Live With Joy

Only what we give away
Enriches us from day to day,
For not in getting but in giving
Is found the lasting joy of living.
For no one ever had a part
In sharing treasures of the heart
Who did not feel the impact of
The magic mystery of God's love.
For love alone can make us kind
And give us joy and peace of mind,
So live with joy unselfishly
And you'll be blessed abundantly.

Help Yourself to Happiness

Everybody, everywhere
   seeks happiness, it's true,
But finding it and keeping it
   seem difficult to do.
Difficult because we think
   that happiness is found
Only in the places where
   wealth and fame abound.
And so we go on searching
   in palaces of pleasure
Seeking recognition
   and monetary treasure,
Unaware that happiness
   is just a state of mind
Within the reach of everyone
   who takes time to be kind.
For in making others happy
   we will be happy, too,
For the happiness you give away
   returns to shine on you.

The only way to multiply happiness is to divide it.
Paul Scherer

Adversity Can Distress Us or Bless Us

The way we use adversity
is strictly our own choice,
For in God's hands adversity
can make the heart rejoice.
For everything God sends to us,
no matter in what form,
Is sent with plan and purpose,
for by the fierceness of a storm
The atmosphere is changed and cleared
and the earth is washed and clean
And the high winds of adversity
can make restless souls serene.
And while it's very difficult
for mankind to understand
God's intentions and His purpose
and the workings of His hand,
If we observe the miracles
that happen every day
We cannot help but be convinced
that in His wondrous way
God makes what seemed unbearable
and painful and distressing,
Easily acceptable
when we view it as a blessing.

On the timberline of the mountain, where the storms beat in full fury, we find the sturdiest of trees, the hearty veterans of ten thousand blasts. Adversity is hard to bear, but it tries the soul and strengthens it.

Author Unknown

No Favor Do I Seek Today

I come not to ask, to plead, or implore You,
I just come to tell You how much I adore You,
And to kneel in Your Presence makes me feel blest
For I know that You know all my needs best.
And it fills me with joy just to linger with You
As my soul You replenish and my heart You renew,
For prayer is much more than just asking for things—
It's the peace and contentment that quietness brings.
So thank You again for Your mercy and love
And for making me heir to Your kingdom above!

"My presence will go with you, and I will give you rest."
                                        Exodus 33:14

Be of Good Cheer

Cheerful thoughts like sunbeams
   lighten up the darkest fears
For when the heart is happy
   there's just no time for tears.
For the nature of our attitude
   toward circumstantial things
Determines our acceptance
   of the problems that life brings,
And since fear and dread and worry
   cannot help in any way,
It's much healthier and happier
   to be cheerful every day.
For when the heart is cheerful
   it cannot be filled with fear,
And without fear the way ahead
   seems more distinct and clear.
And we realize there's nothing
   we need ever face alone,
For our Heavenly Father loves us
   and our problems are His own.

Give us, O give us, the man who sings at his work! Be his occupation what it may, he is equal to any of those who follow the same pursuit in silent sullenness. He will do more in the same time—he will do it better—he will persevere longer.

Carlyle

So Many Reasons to Love the Lord

Thank You, God, for little things
    that come unexpectedly
To brighten up a dreary day
    that dawned so dismally.
Thank You, God, for sending
    a happy thought my way
To blot out my depression
    on a disappointing day.
Thank You, God, for brushing
    the dark clouds from my mind
And leaving only sunshine
    and joy of heart behind.
Oh, God, the list is endless
    of things to thank You for
But I take them all for granted
    and unconsciously ignore
That everything I think or do,
    each movement that I make,
Each measured rhythmic heartbeat,
    each breath of life I take
Is something You have given me
    for which there is no way
For me in all my smallness
    to in any way repay.

Thou who hast given so much to me, give one thing more—a grateful heart.

George Herbert

Start Today With a Smile

Happiness is something that is never far away,
It's as close as the things we do and we say.
So start out today with a smile on your face
And make this old world a happier place.

Happiness comes of the capacity to feel deeply, to enjoy simply, to think freely, to risk life, to be needed.

Storm Jameson

The Joy of Understanding

Not money or gifts or material things
But understanding and the joy that it brings
Can change this old world and its selfish ways
And put goodness and mercy back into our days.

*Real joy comes not from ease or riches or from the praise of men,
but from doing something worthwhile.*

Wilfred T. Grenfell

He Asks So Little and Gives So Much

What must I do to insure peace of mind?
Is the answer I'm seeking too hard to find?
How can I know what God wants me to be?
How can I tell what's expected of me?
Where can I go for guidance and aid
To help me correct the errors I've made?
The answer is found in doing three things,
And great is the gladness that doing them brings.
Do justice, love kindness, walk humbly with God,
For with these three things as your rule and your rod
All things worth having are yours to achieve
If you follow God's Word and have faith to believe!

If you have not often felt the joy of doing a kind act, you have neglected much, and most of all yourself.

A. Neilen

What Has Been Is What Will Be

Today my soul is reaching out
For something that's unknown,
I cannot grasp or fathom it
For it's known to God alone.
I cannot hold or harness it
Or put it into form,
For it's as uncontrollable
As the wind before the storm.
I know not where it came from
Or whither it will go,
For it's as inexplicable
As the restless winds that blow.
And like the wind it too will pass
And leave nothing more behind
Than the memory of a mystery
That blew across my mind.

But like the wind it will return
To keep reminding me
That everything that has been
Is what again will be,
For there is nothing that is new
Beneath God's timeless sun,
And present, past, and future
Are all molded into one.
And east and west and north and south
The same wind keeps on blowing,
While rivers run on endlessly
Yet the sea's not overflowing.
And the restless, unknown longing
Of my searching soul won't cease
Until God comes in glory
And my soul at last finds peace.

What Is Prayer?

Is it measured words that are memorized,
Forcefully said and dramatized,
Offered with pomp and with arrogant pride
In words unmatched to the feelings inside?
No . . . prayer is so often just words unspoken
Whispered in tears by a heart that is broken,
For God is already deeply aware
Of the burdens we find too heavy to bear.
So all we need do is to seek Him in prayer
And without a word He will help us to bear
Our trials and troubles—our sickness and sorrow
And show us the way to a brighter tomorrow.
There's no need at all for impressive prayer,
For the minute we seek God He is already there!

Prayer in its simplest definition is merely a wish turned Godward.
Phillips Brooks

Let Not Your Heart Be Troubled

Whenever I am troubled
   and lost in deep despair
I bundle all my troubles up
   and go to God in prayer.
I tell Him I am heartsick
   and lost and lonely, too,
That my mind is deeply burdened
   and I don't know what to do.
But I know He stilled the tempest
   and calmed the angry sea
And I humbly ask if in His love
   He'll do the same for me.
And then I just keep quiet
   and think only thoughts of peace,
And if I abide in stillness
   my restless murmurings cease.

I need not shout my faith. Thrice eloquent are trees and the green listening sod; hushed are the stars, whose power is never spent; the hills are mute, yet how they speak of God.

Charles Hanson Towne

The House of Prayer

Just close your eyes
   and open your heart
And feel your worries
   and cares depart,
Just yield yourself
   to the Father above
And let Him hold you
   secure in His love—
For life on earth
   grows more involved
With endless problems
   that can't be solved—
But God only asks us
   to do our best,
Then He will take over
   and finish the rest—
So when you are tired,
   discouraged, and blue,
There's always one door
   that is open to you—

And that is the door
  to the house of prayer
And you'll find God waiting
  to meet you there,
And the house of prayer
  is no farther away
Than the quiet spot
  where you kneel and pray—
For the heart is a temple
  when God is there
As we place ourselves
  in His loving care,
And He hears every prayer
  and answers each one
When we pray in His name
  "Thy will be done"—
And the burdens that seemed
  too heavy to bear
Are lifted away
  on the wings of prayer.

Patience

And as for that in the good soil, they are those who, hearing the word, hold it fast in an honest and good heart, and bring forth fruit with patience.

Luke 8:15

There Are Blessings in Everything

Blessings come in many guises
That God alone in love devises,
And sickness which we dread so much
Can bring a very healing touch—
For often on the wings of pain
The peace we sought before in vain
Will come to us with sweet surprise
For God is merciful and wise—
And through long hours of tribulation
God gives us time for meditation,
And no sickness can be counted a loss
That teaches us to bear our cross.

Let Your Wish Become a Prayer

Put your dearest wish
  in God's hands today
And discuss it with Him
  as you faithfully pray,
And you can be sure
  your wish will come true
If God feels that your wish
  will be good for you,
For there's no problem too big
  and no question too small,
Just ask God in faith
  and He'll answer them all,
Not always at once,
  so be patient and wait
For God never comes
  too soon or too late.
So trust in His wisdom
  and believe in His Word,
For no prayer's unanswered
  and no prayer's unheard.

Commit your way to the Lord; trust in him, and he will act.
Psalm 37:5

Easier Grows the Way

Looking ahead, the hills seem steep
  and the road rises up to the sky,
But as we near them and start to climb,
  they never seem half as high.
And thinking of work and trouble,
  we worry and hesitate,
But just as soon as we tackle the job,
  the burden becomes less great.
So never a hill, a task, or load,
  a minute, an hour, a day
But as we grow near it and start to climb,
  easier grows the way.

A merry heart goes all the day, a sad tires in a mile.
                                            William Shakespeare

A Prayer for Patience

God, teach me to be patient,
Teach me to go slow,
Teach me how to wait on You
When my way I do not know.
Teach me sweet forbearance
When things do not go right,
So I remain unruffled
When others grow uptight.
Teach me how to quiet
My racing, rising heart,
So I may hear the answer
You are trying to impart.
Teach me to let go, dear God,
And pray undisturbed until
My heart is filled with inner peace
And I learn to know Your will!

Patience and delay achieve more than force and rage.
Jean de La Fontaine

Dark Shadows Fall in the Lives of Us All

Sickness and sorrow
  come to us all,
But through it we grow
  and learn to stand tall,
For trouble is part
  and parcel of life
And no man can grow
  without struggle and strife,
And the more we endure
  with patience and grace
The stronger we grow
  and the more we can face,
And the more we can face,
  the greater our love,
And with love in our hearts
  we are more conscious of
The pain and the sorrow
  in lives everywhere,
So it is through trouble
  that we learn how to share.

God asks no man whether he will accept life. That is not the choice.
You must take it. The only choice is how.

                                   Henry Ward Beecher

Wish Not for Ease

If wishes worked like magic
And plans worked that way, too,
And if everything you wished for,
Whether good or bad for you,
Immediately were granted
With no effort on your part,
You'd experience no fulfillment
Of your spirit or your heart,
For things achieved too easily
Lose their charm and meaning, too,
For it is life's difficulties
And the trial-times we go through
That make us strong in spirit
And endow us with the will
To surmount the insurmountable
And to climb the highest hill.
So wish not for the easy way
To win your heart's desire,
For the joy's in overcoming
And withstanding flood and fire,
For to triumph over trouble
And grow stronger with defeat
Is to win the kind of victory
That will make your life complete.

For anything worth having one must pay the price; and the price is always work, patience, love, self-sacrifice—no paper currency, no promises to pay, but the gold of real service.

John Burroughs

Never Be Discouraged

There is really nothing we need know
   or even try to understand
If we refuse to be discouraged
   and trust God's guiding hand.
So take heart and meet each minute
   with faith in God's great love,
Aware that every day of life
   is controlled by God above.
And never dread tomorrow
   or what the future brings,
Just pray for strength and courage
   and trust God in all things.
So never grow discouraged,
   be patient and just wait,
For God never comes too early
   and He never comes too late!

If seeds in the black earth can turn into such beautiful roses, what might not the heart of man become in its long journey toward the stars?

Gilbert Keith Chesterton

Kindness

So put away all malice and all guile and insincerity and envy and all slander. Like newborn babes, long for the pure spiritual milk, that by it you may grow up to salvation; for you have tasted the kindness of the Lord.

1 Peter 2:1–3

Take Time to Be Kind

Kindness is a virtue
   given by the Lord.
It pays dividends in happiness,
   and joy is its reward,
For if you practice kindness
   in all you say and do,
The Lord will wrap His kindness
   all around your heart and you,
And wrapped within His kindness
   you are sheltered and secure,
And under His direction
   your way is safe and sure.

The Art of Greatness

It's not fortune or fame
Or worldwide acclaim
That makes for true greatness, you'll find—
It's the wonderful art
Of teaching the heart
To always be thoughtful and kind.

The greatest man is he who chooses the right with invincible resolution; who resists the sorest temptations from within and without; who bears the heaviest burdens cheerfully; who is the calmest in storms, and whose reliance on truth, on virtue, on God, is the most unfaltering.

William Ellery Channing

Count Your Gains
and Not Your Losses

As we travel down life's busy road
Complaining of our heavy load,
We often think God's been unfair
And given us much more than our share
Of little daily irritations
And disappointing tribulations.
We count our losses, not our gain,
And remember only tears and pain . . .
And wrapped up in our own despair
We have no time to see or share
Another's load that far outweighs
Our little problems and dismays.
And so we walk with head held low
And little do we guess or know
That someone near us on life's street
Is burdened deeply with defeat . . .
But if we'd but forget our care
And stop in sympathy to share
The burden that our brother carried,
Our mind and heart would be less harried,
And we would feel our load was small,
In fact, we carried no load at all.

Bear one another's burdens, and so fulfil the law of Christ.
Galatians 6:2

Brighten the Corner Where You Are

We cannot all be famous
    or be listed in ''Who's Who,''
But every person great or small
    has important work to do,
For seldom do we realize
    the importance of small deeds
Or to what degree of greatness
    unnoticed kindness leads.
For it's not the big celebrity
    in a world of fame and praise,
But it's doing unpretentiously
    in undistinguished ways
The work that God assigned to us,
    unimportant as it seems,
That makes our task outstanding
    and brings reality to dreams.

So do not sit and idly wish
    for wider, new dimensions
Where you can put in practice
    your many good intentions,
But at the spot God placed you
    begin at once to do
Little things to brighten up
    the lives surrounding you,
For if everybody brightened up
    the spot on which they're standing
By being more considerate
    and a little less demanding,
This dark old world would very soon
    eclipse the evening star
If everybody brightened up
    the corner where they are!

Every Day Is a Reason for Giving,
and Giving Is the Key to Living . . .

So let us give ourselves away,
Not just today but every day,
And remember, a kind and thoughtful deed
Or a hand outstretched in a time of need
Is the rarest of gifts, for it is a part
Not of the purse but a loving heart,
And he who gives of himself will find
True joy of heart and peace of mind.

Kindness has been described in many ways. It is the poetry of the heart, the music of the world. It is a golden chain which binds society together. Kind words produce their own beautiful image in man's soul. Everyone knows the pleasure of receiving a kind look, a warm greeting, a hand held out in time of need. And such gestures can be made at so little expense, yet they bring such dividends to the investor.

The War Cry

Give Us Daily Awareness

On life's busy thoroughfares
We meet with angels unawares,
So, Father, make us kind and wise
So we may always recognize
The blessings that are ours to take,
The friendships that are ours to make
If we but open our heart's door wide
To let the sunshine of love inside,
For God is not in far distant places
But in loving hearts and friendly faces.

The art of awareness is the art of learning how to wake up to the
eternal miracle of life with its limitless possibilities.

Wilfred A. Peterson

Goodness

O how abundant is thy goodness, which thou hast laid up for those who fear thee, and wrought for those who take refuge in thee, in the sight of the sons of men!

Psalm 31:19

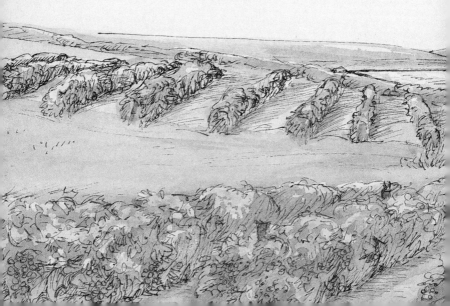

Showers of Blessings

Each day there are showers of blessings
Sent from the Father above,
For God is a great, lavish giver
And there is no end to His love.
His grace is more than sufficient,
His mercy is boundless and deep,
And His infinite blessings are countless,
And all this we're given to keep
If we but seek God and find Him
And ask for a bounteous measure
Of this wholly immeasurable offering
From God's inexhaustible treasure,
For no matter how big man's dreams are,
God's blessings are infinitely more,
For always God's giving is greater
Than what man is asking for.

I Meet God in the Morning

The earth is the Lord's
   and the fulness thereof,
It speaks of His greatness,
   it sings of His love,
And each day at dawning
   I lift my heart high
And raise up my eyes
   to the infinite sky . . .
I see the dew glisten
   in crystal-like splendor
While God, with a touch
   that is gentle and tender,
Wraps up the night
   and softly tucks it away
And hangs out the sun
   to herald a new day,
A day yet unblemished
   by what's gone before,
A chance to begin
   and start over once more,
And all I need do
   is to silently pray,
God, help me and guide me
   and go with me today.

God's gifts put man's best dreams to shame.
Elizabeth Barrett Browning

Wisdom Comes From God

Knowledge comes from learning,
    but wisdom comes from God,
The God who made the universe—
    the sea, the sky, the sod—
The God who makes it possible
    to find miracles each day,
If we but trust His wisdom
    and follow in His way.

The world will never starve for want of wonders.
Gilbert Keith Chesterton

Thank You, God, for Everything

Thank You, God, for everything,
   the big things and the small,
For every good gift comes from God,
   the giver of them all.
And all too often we accept
   without any thanks or praise
The gifts God sends as blessings
   each day in many ways.
First, thank You for the little things
   that often come our way,
The things we take for granted
   but don't mention when we pray,
Then, thank You for the miracles
   we are much too blind to see,
And give us new awareness
   of our many gifts from Thee,
And help us to remember
   that the key to life and living
Is to make each prayer a prayer of thanks
   and every day thanksgiving.

Into all our lives, in many simple, familiar, homely ways, God infuses this element of joy from the surprises of life, which unexpectedly brighten our days, and fill our eyes with light.

Samuel Longfellow

Quit Supposin'

Don't start your day by supposin'
   that trouble is just ahead,
It's better to stop supposin'
   and start with a prayer instead,
And make it a prayer of thanksgiving
   for the wonderful things God has wrought,
Like the beautiful sunrise and sunset,
   God's gifts that are free and not bought.
For what is the use of supposin'
   the dire things that could happen to you
And worrying about some misfortune
   that seldom if ever comes true?
For supposin' the worst things will happen
   only helps to make them come true
And you darken the bright, happy moments
   that the dear Lord has given to you.
So if you desire to be happy
   and get rid of the misery of dread
Just give up supposin' the worst things
   and look for the best things instead.

Let us be of good cheer, remembering that the misfortunes hardest to bear are those which never come.

Amy Lowell

Look on the Sunny Side

There are always two sides,
  the good and the bad,
The dark and the light,
  the sad and the glad,
But in looking back over
  the good and the bad
We're aware of the number
  of good things we've had.
And in counting our blessings
  we find when we're through
We've no reason at all
  to complain or be blue,
So thank God for good things
  He has already done,
And be grateful to Him
  for the battles you've won,

And know that the same God
  who helped you before
Is ready and willing
  to help you once more.
Then with faith in your heart
  reach out for God's hand
And accept what He sends,
  though you can't understand,
For our Father in heaven
  always knows what is best,
And if you trust in His wisdom
  your life will be blessed,
For always remember
  that whatever betide you
You are never alone
  for God is beside you.

God, I Know I Love You

God, I know that I love You
  and I know without a doubt
That Your goodness and mercy
  never run out . . .
I know You forgive me
  for the wrong things I've done,
And I know that to save me
  You sent Your own Son . . .
I know I should thank You
  and thank You, I do . . .
I shall praise and adore You
  all my days through.

God has put something noble and good into every heart which His hand created.

Mark Twain

Where Can We Find Him?

Where can we find The Holy One?
Where can we see His only Son?
The Wise Men asked, and we're asking still,
Where can we find this Man of goodwill?
Is He far away in some distant place,
Ruling unseen from His throne of grace?
Is there nothing on earth that man can see
To give him proof of eternity?

It's true we have never looked on God's face,
But His likeness shines forth from every place,
For the hand of God is everywhere
Along life's busy thoroughfare,
And His presence can be felt and seen
Right in the midst of our daily routine,
The things we touch and see and feel
Are what make God so very real.

I love to think of nature as an unlimited broadcasting station, through which God speaks to us every hour, if we will only tune in.
George Washington Carver

Faithfulness

Steadfast love and faithfulness will meet; righteousness and peace will kiss each other. Faithfulness will spring up from the ground, and righteousness will look down from the sky. Yea, the Lord will give what is good, and our land will yield its increase. Righteousness will go before him, and make his footsteps a way.

Psalm 85:10–13

Mover of Mountains

Faith is a force that is greater
   than knowledge or power or skill,
And the darkest defeat turns to triumph
   if we trust in God's wisdom and will.
For faith is a mover of mountains,
   there's nothing man cannot achieve
If he has the courage to try it
   and then has the faith to believe.

Never Borrow Sorrow
From Tomorrow

Deal only with the present,
Never step into tomorrow,
For God asks us just to trust Him
And to never borrow sorrow,
For the future is not ours to know
And it may never be,
So let us live and give our best
And give it lavishly,
For to meet tomorrow's troubles
Before they are even ours
Is to anticipate the Savior
And to doubt His all-wise powers.
So let us be content to solve
Our problems one by one,
Asking nothing of tomorrow
Except Thy will be done.

One of the most tragic things I know about human nature is that all of us tend to put off living. We are all dreaming of some magical rose garden over the horizon—instead of enjoying the roses that are blooming outside our windows today.

Dale Carnegie

The Future Is Yours

The future is yours,
it belongs to you,
And with faith in God
and in yourself, too,
No hill's too high,
no mountain's too tall,
For with faith in the Lord
you can conquer them all.
And all that you wish for
that is honest and true
The Lord will certainly
give to you,
Not always the way
you most desire,
But He always gives
what you most require.
So accept what He sends,
be it bitter or sweet,
For God knows best
what makes life complete.

Success is to be measured not so much by the position that one has reached in life as by the obstacles which he has overcome while trying to succeed.

Booker T. Washington

God, Are You There?

I'm way down here!
   You're way up there!
Are You sure You can hear
   my faint, faltering prayer?
For I'm so unsure
   of just how to pray,
To tell You the truth, God,
   I don't know what to say.
I just know I am lonely
   and vaguely disturbed,
Bewildered and restless,
   confused and perturbed,
And they tell me that prayer
   helps to quiet the mind
And to unburden the heart
   for in stillness we find
A newborn assurance
   that Someone does care
And Someone does answer
   each small, sincere prayer!

Now faith is the assurance of things hoped for, the conviction of things not seen.

Hebrews 11:1

Your Life Will Be Blessed
if You Look for the Best

It's easy to grow downhearted
   when nothing goes your way,
It's easy to be discouraged
   when you have a troublesome day,
But trouble is only a challenge
   to spur you on to achieve
The best that God has to offer
   if you have the faith to believe!

Even the woodpecker owes his success to the fact that he uses his head and keeps pecking away until he finishes the job he starts.
Coleman Cox

Climb Till Your Dream Comes True

Often your tasks will be many,
And more than you think you can do,
Often the road will be rugged
And the hills insurmountable, too,
But always remember, the hills ahead
Are never as steep as they seem,
And with faith in your heart start upward
And climb till you reach your dream.
For nothing in life that is worthy
Is ever too hard to achieve
If you have the courage to try it
And you have the faith to believe.
For faith is a force that is greater
Than knowledge or power or skill
And many defeats turn to triumph
If you trust in God's wisdom and will.
For faith is a mover of mountains,
There's nothing that God cannot do,
So start out today with faith in your heart
And climb till your dream comes true!

By faith you can move mountains; but the important thing is, not to move the mountains, but to have faith.

Arthur Clutton-Brock

Let Go and Let God!

When you're troubled and worried
    and sick at heart
And your plans are upset,
    and your world falls apart,
Remember God's ready
    and waiting to share
The burden you find
    much too heavy to bear.
So with faith, let go
    and let God lead the way
Into a brighter
    and less-troubled day,
For God has a plan
    for everyone
If we learn to pray,
    ''Thy will be done.''
For nothing in life
    is without God's design
And each life is fashioned
    by the hand that's Divine.

Let not your hearts be troubled; believe in God, believe also in me.
John 14:1

If We But Believe

If we put our problems
  in God's hand,
There is nothing
  we need understand . . .
It is enough
  to just believe
That what we need
  we will receive.

When God allows a burden to be put upon you, He will put His
own arm underneath you to help.

Author Unknown

Daily Prayers Are Heaven's Stairs

The stairway rises heaven high,
The steps are dark and steep,
In weariness we climb them
As we stumble, fall, and weep,
And many times we falter
Along the path of prayer,
Wondering if You hear us
And if You really care.
Oh, give us some assurance,
Restore our faith anew,
So we can keep on climbing
The stairs of prayer to You,
For we are weak and wavering,
Uncertain and unsure,
And only meeting You in prayer
Can help us to endure
All life's trials and troubles,
Its sickness, pain, and sorrow,
And give us strength and courage
To face and meet tomorrow!

Be strong, and let your heart take courage, all you who wait for the Lord!

Psalm 31:24

Gentleness

Brethren, if a man is overtaken in any trespass, you who are spiritual should restore him in a spirit of gentleness. Look to yourself, lest you too be tempted. Bear one another's burdens, and so fulfil the law of Christ.

Galatians 6:1, 2

Smile

When you do what you do
    with a will and a smile,
Everything that you do
    will seem twice as worthwhile,
And when you walk down the street,
    life will seem twice as sweet
If you smile at the people
    you happen to meet,
For when you smile, it is true,
    folks will smile back at you . . .
So do what you do
    with a will and a smile,
And whatever you do
    will be twice as worthwhile.

The Language of the Heart

Just like a sunbeam brightens the sky,
A smile on the face of a passerby
Can make a drab and crowded street
A pleasant place where two smiles meet.

The beauty of the sunbeam lies partly in the fact that God does not keep it; He gives it away to us all.

David Swing

Somebody Cares

Somebody cares and always will,
The world forgets but God loves you still,
You cannot go beyond His love
No matter what you're guilty of,
For God forgives until the end,
He is your faithful, loyal friend,
And though you try to hide your face
There is no shelter any place
That can escape His watchful eye,
For on the earth and in the sky
He's ever-present and always there
To take you in His tender care
And bind the wounds and mend the breaks
When all the world around forsakes.
Somebody cares and loves you still
And God is the Someone who always will.

God deals with us whether in sickness or in health, whether in prosperity or adversity, whether in good or in evil days, whether in life or in death, not according to our merit but according to His mercy and love.

Albert J. Penner

God's Jewels

We watch the rich and famous
Bedecked in precious jewels,
Enjoying earthly pleasures,
Defying moral rules.
And in our mood of discontent
We sink into despair
And long for earthly riches
And feel cheated of our share.
But stop these idle musings,
God has stored up for you
Treasures that are far beyond
Earth's jewels and riches, too,
For never, never discount
What God has promised man
If he will walk in meekness
And accept God's flawless plan,
For if we heed His teachings
As we journey through the years,
We'll find the richest jewels of all
Are crystalized from tears.

Blessed are the meek, for they shall inherit the earth.
Matthew 5:5

Good Morning, God!

You are ushering in another day
Untouched and freshly new
So here I come to ask You, God,
If You'll renew me, too.
Forgive the many errors
That I made yesterday
And let me try again, dear God,
To walk closer in Thy way.
But, Father, I am well aware
I can't make it on my own,
So take my hand and hold it tight
For I can't walk alone!

We may imitate the Deity in all His attributes; but mercy is the only one in which we can pretend to equal Him. We cannot, indeed, give like God; but surely we may forgive like Him.

Laurence Sterne

Self-control

A man without self-control is like a city broken into and left without walls.

Proverbs 25:28

Your Choice

God gives all men a choice,
They can rebel or they can rejoice,
And trouble can mend or mar your life
Or fill it with sunshine or sink it in strife.

How Great the Yield
From a Fertile Field

The farmer plows through the fields of green
And the blade of the plow is sharp and keen,
But the seed must be sown to bring forth grain,
For nothing is born without suffering and pain,
And God never plows in the soul of man
Without intention and purpose and plan.
So whenever you feel the plow's sharp blade
Let not your heart be sorely afraid,
For, like the farmer, God chooses a field
From which He expects an excellent yield,
So rejoice though your heart is broken in two,
God seeks to bring forth a rich harvest in you.

Humble yourselves therefore under the mighty hand of God, that in due time he may exalt you. Cast all your anxieties on him, for he cares about you.

1 Peter 5:6, 7

A Sure Way to a Happy Day

Happiness is something we create in our mind,
It's not something we search for and so seldom find,
It's just waking up and beginning the day
by counting our blessings and kneeling to pray,
It's giving up thoughts that breed discontent
And accepting what comes as a gift heaven-sent,
It's giving up wishing for things we have not
And making the best of whatever we've got,
It's knowing that life is determined for us,
And pursuing our tasks without fret, fume, or fuss,
For it's by completing what God gives us to do
That we find real contentment and happiness, too.

The only ones among you who will be really happy are those who will have sought and found how to serve.

Albert Schweitzer

Worry No More!
God Knows the Score!

Have you ever been caught
    in a web you didn't weave,
Involved in conditions
    that are hard to believe?
Have you felt you must speak
    and explain and deny
A story that's groundless
    or a small, whispered lie?
Have you ever heard rumors
    you would like to refute
Or some telltale gossip
    you would like to dispute?
Well, don't be upset,
    for God knows the score
And with God as your judge
    you need worry no more,

For men may misjudge you
  but God's verdict is fair,
For He looks deep inside
  and He is clearly aware
Of every small detail
  in your pattern of living
And always He's lenient
  and fair and forgiving—
And knowing that God
  is your judge and your jury
Frees you completely
  from man's falseness and fury,
And secure in this knowledge
  let your thoughts rise above
Man's small, shallow judgments
  that are so empty of
God's goodness and greatness
  in judging all men
And forget ugly rumors
  and be happy again.

This Too Will Pass Away

If I can endure for this minute
Whatever is happening to me,
No matter how heavy my heart is
Or how dark the moment may be,
If I can remain calm and quiet
With all my world crashing about me,
Secure in the knowledge God loves me
When everyone else seems to doubt me,
If I can keep on believing
What I know in my heart to be true,
That darkness will fade with the morning
And that this will pass away, too,
Then nothing in life can defeat me,
For as long as this knowledge remains
I can suffer whatever is happening
For I know God will break all the chains
That are binding me tight in the darkness
And trying to fill me with fear,
For there is no night without dawning
And I know that my morning is near.

To reach the port of heaven we must sail, sometimes with the wind and sometimes against it—but we must sail, not drift or lie at anchor.

Oliver Wendell Holmes

Lives Distressed Cannot Be Blessed

Refuse to be discouraged,
Refuse to be distressed,
For when we are despondent
Our life cannot be blessed,
For doubt and fear and worry
Close the door to faith and prayer,
And there's no room for blessings
When we're lost in deep despair,
So remember when we're troubled
With uncertainty and doubt
It is best to tell our Father
What our fear is all about.
For unless we seek His guidance
When troubled times arise,
We are bound to make decisions
That are twisted and unwise,
But when we view our problems
Through the eyes of God above,
Misfortunes turn to blessings
And hatred turns to love.

The voluntary path to cheerfulness, if our spontaneous cheerfulness be lost, is to sit up cheerfully, and act and speak as if cheerfulness were already there.

William James

Seek Ye First the Kingdom of God

Life is a mixture
   of sunshine and rain,
Good things and bad things,
   pleasure and pain.
We can't have all sunshine,
   but it's certainly true
There is never a cloud
   the sun doesn't shine through.
So always remember
   that whatever betide you
The power of God
   is always beside you
And if friends disappoint you
   and plans go astray
And nothing works out
   in just the right way,
And you feel you have failed
   in achieving your goal,
And that life wrongly placed you
   in an unfitting role,
Take heart and stand tall
   and think who you are,

For God is your Father
and no one can bar
Or keep you from reaching
your desired success,
Or withhold the joy
that is yours to possess,
For with God on your side
it matters not who
Is working to keep
life's good things from you,
For you need nothing more
than God's guidance and love
To insure you the things
that you're most worthy of.
So trust in His wisdom
and follow His ways,
And be not concerned
with the world's empty praise,
But seek first His kingdom
and you will possess
The world's greatest riches
which is true happiness.

Thanks to each and every one
Who has ever played a part
By sharing and caring
And thus preparing
Joy for another's heart.

VJR